# A Taste of MAINE
# APPETIZERS

BLUE HILL
Photo: ©Gary Stanley

## Crab Parmesan Canapés

| | |
|---|---|
| 12 | slices white bread, crusts discarded and bread cut into 4 triangles |
| 1 | cup fresh lump crab meat, picked over |
| 2/3 | cup mayonnaise |
| 2/3 | cup freshly grated Parmesan cheese |
| 4 | green onions, chopped fine |
| 1 | teaspoon fresh lemon juice, or to taste |
| | Salt and freshly ground pepper to taste |

*Preheat oven to 400°. Toast bread on a baking sheet in oven until golden, about 5 minutes. In a bowl stir together remaining ingredients with salt and pepper to taste. Spread crabmeat mixture on toast triangles and arrange on baking sheet. (Canapés may be assembled 30 minutes in advance.) Bake canapés in middle of oven until puffed, about 10 minutes. Makes 48 canapés.*

## Baked Stuffed Clams

| | |
|---|---|
| 12 | large clam shells, boiled and cleaned |
| 1 | cup clam juice |
| 1 | cup chopped clams |
| 1 | tablespoon bacon fat |
| 2 | tablespoons butter |
| 1 | teaspoon chopped garlic |
| 1 | teaspoon oregano |
| 1 | tablespoon chopped parsley |
| 3 | tablespoons flour |
| 2 | cups bread crumbs |

*Preheat oven to 400°. In a skillet, heat the bacon fat and butter with the garlic and oregano. Add the flour to make a roux. Cook 1 minute stirring constantly. Add the clam juice and bring to a boil. Add the chopped clams and parsley. Season with salt and pepper. Cook 1 minute. Add the bread crumbs. Spoon into clam shells. Bake 15-20 minutes until tops are browned and stuffing is heated through. Makes 12.*

## Baked Brie with Cranberries and Almonds

Pastry Ingredients:

| | |
|---|---|
| 3/4 | cup all-purpose flour |
| 1/4 | cup butter, softened |
| 1 | (3-ounce) package cream cheese, softened |

Filling Ingredients:

| | |
|---|---|
| 1 | (8-ounce) 4 1/4-inch diameter round Brie cheese (do not remove rind) |
| 3 | tablespoons cranberry sauce |
| 3 | tablespoons chopped almonds, toasted |

Topping Ingredients:

| | |
|---|---|
| 1 | large egg |
| 1 | teaspoon water |

*Combine flour, butter and cream cheese in large mixer bowl. Beat at low speed, scraping bowl often, until mixture leaves sides of bowl and forms a ball (2 to 3 minutes). Divide dough in half; wrap in plastic food wrap. Refrigerate until firm (1 hour). Preheat oven to 400°F. Roll each half of dough on lightly floured surface to 1/8-inch thickness. Cut an 8-inch circle from each half (save dough scraps for decoration). Place 1 circle on ungreased baking sheet. Place Brie on center of pastry circle. Spread cranberry sauce over top of Brie cheese; sprinkle with toasted almonds. Top with other pastry circle. Pinch edges of pastry to seal. Flute edges as desired. Decorate top with small pastry cutouts. Beat egg with water in small bowl; brush top and sides of pastry. Bake for 15 to 20 minutes or until golden brown. Remove from baking sheet immediately. Let stand 30 minutes to allow cheese to set. Cut into small wedges. Serve with apple slices and crackers. Makes 8 servings.*

# Scallop Blankets

| | |
|---|---|
| 1/2 | pound Maine sea scallops (if very large, cut in half) |
| 2 | tablespoons dry sherry |
| 1/2 | teaspoon sugar |
| 1/2 | teaspoon salt |
| 6 | slices bacon |
| 6 | water chestnuts, halved |
| 2 | green onions, sliced into 1-inch pieces |

*In a small bowl, stir together the sherry and sugar. Add the scallops and marinate for 30-40 minutes. Remove scallops from marinade and sprinkle with salt. Center a scallop (or 1/2), water chestnut, and green onion slice on a slice (or half slice) of bacon. Wrap and secure with a toothpick. Arrange on a broiling pan. Broil for 10 minutes, turning once, until bacon is golden and scallops are cooked. Serves 4*

## Cheese and Herb Twists

| | |
|---|---|
| 6 | ounces white Cheddar cheese, finely grated |
| 3/4 | teaspoon dried thyme |
| 3/4 | teaspoon dried sage |
| 1/2 | teaspoon freshly ground black pepper |
| 1 | sheet frozen puff pastry, thawed |

*Mix first 4 ingredients in a small bowl. Roll out puff pastry on a floured work surface to an 18" x 10" rectangle. Spread 1/2 of pastry with 1/3 of the cheese mixture. Fold other half over cheese sprinkled half (now you have a 9 x 10" rectangle). Roll out into an 18" x 10" rectangle. Repeat this procedure twice ending with an 18" x 10" rectangle. Place on a cookie sheet and chill 30 minutes. Preheat oven to 425°. Cut rectangle in half forming 2 (9" x 10" rectangles). Crosswise, cut each into strips about 1/2 inch wide. Twist each strip 3 or 4 times and place on baking sheets lined with parchment paper. Dab ends with water and press onto parchment paper to keep from untwisting. Bake in preheated oven for 10 minutes. Let cool in pans. Serve warm. Makes 24-36.*

## Warm Maine Lobster Dip

| | |
|---|---|
| 2 | 8-ounce packages low fat cream cheese |
| 2 | cups cooked Maine lobster meat |
| 2 | tablespoons finely chopped onion |
| 1 | tablespoon fresh horseradish |
| 1 | teaspoon Worcestershire sauce |
| | Hot pepper sauce to taste |
| | Milk, as needed, to thin a bit, if desired |
| 1/4 | cup chopped walnuts |

*Soften the cream cheese, and cut the lobster meat into bite size pieces. Stir all the ingredients together, adjusting the consistency, as wished. Place into an ovenproof dish and refrigerate for several hours. When ready to serve, bake uncovered at 375° F. for 25 minutes until bubbly. Serve with crackers or chips.*

## Lobster Pate

| | |
|---|---|
| 2 | fresh 1 1/2 pound lobsters |
| 1 | pound cream cheese |
| 1/2 | cup sour cream |
| 1 | tablespoon each fresh parsley, chives, tarragon and chervil, minced |
| 2 | tablespoons lemon juice |
| | Salt and pepper to taste |

*Steam the lobsters. Let cool and pick out the meat. Combine all ingredients in a blender. Blend until all is mixed well. If too thick, add some sour cream. Season. Pour into a mold and chill thoroughly. Serve with crackers. Serves 10-12.*

## Muffin 'Crabbies'

| | |
|---|---|
| 6 | English muffins |
| 1 | pound lump crabmeat (picked well for shells) |
| 3 | jars cheese spread, softened |
| | Salt and pepper to taste |

*Mix crabmeat, cheese, and seasoning together and spread on split muffin halves. Place under the broiler (cheese side up) until just browned lightly. Cut each muffin half into 4 little "pizza slice" like pieces. Serve immediately.*

LOBSTERS
Photo: ©Mike Jones

# Stuffed Mushrooms

| 1 | pound large white mushrooms |
| 1 | package Stouffers frozen spinach soufflé |
| 3 | tablespoons grated Parmesan cheese |

*Clean mushrooms; slightly defrost the soufflé and spoon into mushroom caps. Top with Parmesan cheese. Bake in a preheated 375° oven for 20 minutes or until hot and bubbly.*

## Apple Curry Chutney with Ham Roll-ups

1   (8-ounce) package cream cheese, softened
1/2   cup apple curry chutney
1   large green onion, chopped
8   (8-inch) soft-taco sized flour tortillas
6   (1-ounce) slices ham

*Combine cream cheese, chutney and green onion in small bowl; mix well. Spread about 1/4 cup chutney mixture over each tortilla; top with slice of ham. Roll up; wrap tightly in plastic wrap. Refrigerate for 30 minutes. Remove plastic wrap; cut each roll into 6 slices. Makes 48 pieces.*

## Baked Spinach and Artichoke Dip

1   (14-ounce) can artichoke hearts, drained and chopped
1   (10-ounce) package frozen chopped spinach, thawed and drained
1   (8-ounce) container lowfat plain yogurt
1   cup (4-ounces) shredded part-skim Mozzarella cheese
1/4   cup chopped green onion
1   garlic clove, minced
2   tablespoons chopped red bell pepper

*Combine all ingredients except red pepper and mix well. Pour mixture into 1-quart casserole dish or 9-inch pie plate. Bake at 350° for 20 to 25 minutes or until heated through and sprinkle with red peppers. Serve with toasted bread or whole grain crackers.*

## Smoked Oyster Dip

1   tablespoon minced onion
1/2   pound fresh mushrooms, chopped
2   tablespoons butter
1   3-ounce can smoked oysters, drained and chopped
1   3-ounce package cream cheese, softened
1/2   cup sour cream
1   teaspoon seasoning salt
1/4   teaspoon pepper
   Dash hot pepper sauce

*Saute onion and mushrooms in butter. Combine oysters, cream cheese, sour cream and seasonings. Stir in the onions and mushrooms. Serve hot or cold with crackers or chips.*

## Crab Hors D'oeuvre

1   can frozen or canned crab, drained well
1   8-ounce package cream cheese
1 1/2   tablespoons Worcestershire sauce
2/3   teaspoon lemon juice
1 1/2   tablespoons mayonnaise
   Minced onion
2/3   cup bottled chili sauce

*Mix and spread on plate. Refrigerate for at least 3 hours. Just before serving, spread chili sauce over mixture. Serve with crackers or chips.*

# A Taste of MAINE
# SOUPS &
# SALADS

BERNARD BOATS IN FOG
Photo: ©Gary Stanley

# Lobster Bisque

| | |
|---|---|
| 2 | 1-pound Maine lobsters |
| 2 | tablespoons butter |
| 2 | cups lobster stock |
| 4 | cups cream |
| 1/4 | cup dry sherry |
| | Salt and pepper to taste |

*Cook lobsters in boiling water for 25 minutes. Remove meat from the body, claws, and legs of the lobsters. Reserve lobster shells for stock. Follow stock recipe. Sauté lobster meat in butter for three minutes, over medium heat. Add stock, cream, sherry, salt, and pepper. Cook over low heat until hot. Do not let bisque boil. Serves 4-6.*

# Spinach Salad with Hot Bacon Dressing

| | |
|---|---|
| 1 | pound fresh baby spinach leaves, cleaned and dried |
| 6 | slices bacon, diced |
| 1/4 | cup white vinegar |
| 1/4 | cup sugar |

*Fry bacon in a skillet over medium heat until crisp. Remove from heat and pour off half the fat. leaving about 1/4 cup drippings. Stir in the vinegar and sugar and bring to a boil. Put spinach in a large heatproof salad bowl. Pour the dressing over the spinach and toss lightly. Serve immediately. Serves 6.*

# Panzanella
## Bread and Tomato Salad

| | |
|---|---|
| 3 | pounds ripe, red and/or yellow tomatoes, cut into chunks |
| 1 | cup torn basil leaves |
| 1 | cup chopped parsley |
| 1/4 | cup minced red onion |
| 1/4 | cup finely chopped red bell pepper |
| 1 | teaspoon coarse salt |
| 3 | cups day old French or Italian bread, cut into 2" squares (no crusts) |
| 3 | tablespoons olive oil |
| 2 | tablespoons minced garlic |
| 2 | tablespoons slivered garlic |
| 1/2 | cup plus 2 tablespoons olive oil |
| 3 | tablespoons red wine vinegar |
| 1 | teaspoon salt |
| 1 | teaspoon cracked black pepper |

*Toss the following together and let sit at room temperature at least 15 minutes: tomato chunks, basil, parsley, onion, sweet pepper and coarse salt. Make croutons by tossing together the bread, oil, and garlic together until bread is evenly coated. Place croutons on cookie sheet and toast 20 minutes at 375 degrees, until golden. Then toss these together with the tomatoes and juices they have created.*

*Dressing:*
*Mix in a bowl the slivered garlic, oil, red wine vinegar, salt and cracked pepper. Gently mix this into the crouton and tomato mixture. Divide into 8 bowls and serve.*

CADILLAC MOUNTAIN
Photo: ©Robert Villani

# New England Clam Chowder

| | |
|---|---|
| 3 cups drained, chopped clams (reserve broth) | 2 cups diced potatoes |
| 4 ounces diced bacon | Clam juice |
| 1 cup finely chopped onion | 2 cups light cream |
| | Salt & pepper taste |

*Fry bacon until crisp. Remove from pan. Add onion to remaining fat in pan and cook three minutes. Add potatoes. Add enough clam broth to just cover the potatoes. Cover and simmer until potatoes are tender. Add clams and simmer 5 minutes. Add the cream and heat but do not boil Season to taste. Serves 4-6*

## Spinach Salad with Blueberries and Chicken

| | |
|---|---|
| 4 | 6-ounce boneless chicken breasts |
| 8 | cups torn, fresh spinach |
| 2 | cups fresh or thawed Maine wild blueberries |
| 1 | tablespoon finely sliced red onion |
| 1 | tablespoon sunflower seeds |
| 1/2 | tablespoon toasted sesame seeds |
| 2 | tablespoons vegetable oil |
| 2 | tablespoons vinegar |
| 4 1/2 | teaspoons sugar |
| 1/2 | teaspoon dill weed |
| | Salt and pepper to taste |

*Grill chicken until completely cooked. Set aside and cool. Then slice chicken into strips. In a salad bowl, combine the spinach, blueberries, onion, sunflower seeds, and sesame seeds. In a container with cover combine the remaining ingredients; shake well. Place chicken in a bowl with greens and pour dressing over salad and gently toss. Serves 4-6*

## Cucumber Salad

| | |
|---|---|
| 4 | medium-sized cucumbers |
| 1 | tablespoon coarse salt |
| 1/4 | cup sugar |
| 1 | cup white vinegar |
| 3 | tablespoons chopped fresh dill |

*Peel cucumbers and slice thinly. Place in a bowl and sprinkle over the salt. Mix and set aside for 15 minutes. Place cucumbers in a colander and let drain for several hours. Rinse with water and squeeze the cucumbers to get rid of as much moisture as possible. Add sugar, vinegar and freshly chopped dill. Serves 6.*

## Maine Fish Chowder

| | |
|---|---|
| 1/4 | pound salt pork, diced |
| 4 | cups diced raw potatoes |
| 2 | small onions, peeled & sliced |
| 2 | teaspoons salt |
| 3 | pounds white fleshed fish, such as haddock |
| 2 | cups scalded milk |
| 1 | teaspoon butter |
| 1/4 | teaspoon pepper |

*Fry salt pork to render all fat in a heavy kettle and then remove. Add potatoes, onions, and 1/2 teaspoon salt. Cover with hot water and cook over medium heat, covered, 15 minutes, until potatoes are just tender. Do not overcook. Meanwhile, cut fish into large chunks and put into another saucepan. Add boiling water to cover and 1 1/2 teaspoons salt. Cook slowly, covered, until fish is fork tender, about 15 minutes. Remove from heat. Strain and reserve liquid. Remove any bones from fish. Add fish and strained liquid to potato-onion mixture. Pour in milk and heat through, about 5 minutes. Stir in butter and pepper. Serve at once. Serves 4 to 6.*

## Old Fashioned Potato Salad

| | |
|---|---|
| 1 | cup mayonnaise |
| 1 | teaspoon dry mustard |
| 1/4 | teaspoon pepper |
| 4 | medium Maine potatoes, cooked and diced |
| 4 | hard-boiled eggs, chopped |
| 1 | cup celery, chopped |
| 1/4 | cup onion, chopped |

*Mix mayonnaise, mustard and pepper in a large bowl. Add remaining ingredients; mix lightly. Refrigerate. Makes 8 servings.*

# Lobster Salad

| | | | | |
|---|---|---|---|---|
| 2 | cups mayonnaise | | 6 | green onions, chopped |
| 1/4 | cup chili paste | | 1/2 | cup finely chopped green bell pepper |
| 1/4 | teaspoon finely chopped garlic | | | Salt and pepper to taste |
| 1 | finely diced shallot | | 1 1/4 | pounds Maine lobster |
| 1 | cup lightly whipped heavy cream | | 1 | lemon, cut into wedges |
| 1 | tablespoon lemon juice | | | |

*Steam the lobster for 10 minutes. Shock the lobster in ice water and remove. Split the lobster in have length ways. Set aside in refrigerator.*

*Sauce: Lightly whip the cream. In a large bowl fold all the ingredients until well mixed. Taste and season. Allow the sauce to chill in refrigerator. Place the sauce in a small serving bowl. Place a half of the lobster on each of 2 chilled plates with the lemon wedge.  Serve with the sauce. Serves 2.*

## Broccoli Salad

3       cups broccoli flowerets
1       cup raisins
1       small onion, finely chopped
8       strips bacon, fried and crumbled
1       cup Cheddar cheese
1       cup sunflower seeds

Dressing:
1       cup mayonnaise
3       tablespoons vinegar
1/4     cup sugar
*Mix all ingredients well.*

*Mix together the broccoli flowerets, raisins, onion, bacon, cheese and sunflower seeds. Gently stir in the dressing. Cover and refrigerate until ready to serve. Serves 4-6.*

## Curried Pumpkin Soup

1       tablespoon vegetable oil
1       onion, chopped
1       cup unsweetened applesauce
1       tablespoon granulated sugar
1       teaspoon curry powder
1       teaspoon ground cumin
1/2     teaspoon ground ginger
1/2     teaspoon salt
1/4     teaspoon ground cardamom
1/4     teaspoon ground black pepper
1       (15-ounce) can pure pumpkin
1       (14.5-ounce) can low sodium chicken broth
1       (12-ounce) can nonfat evaporated milk

*Heat a large, heavy-bottomed pan over medium heat. Add oil and sauté onion until soft, about 7 minutes. Stir in applesauce, sugar, curry powder, cumin, ginger, salt, cardamom and pepper; cook for 5 more minutes, stirring frequently. Add pumpkin and chicken broth; stir well. Bring to a boil, cover and reduce heat. Gently simmer for 20 minutes, stirring occasionally. Remove from heat and stir in evaporated milk. Process in batches in a blender or in the pot with an immersion blender until smooth. Reheat, if needed, over low heat. Serve warm. Serves 6.*

## Hot German Potato Salad

1 1/2   pounds Maine potatoes, cooked and cut up
1       medium onion, sliced thinly
6       strips bacon, cooked and crumbled
1/3     cup vinegar
2       tablespoons flour
1 1/2   teaspoon salt
1/2     cup chopped parsley
1/2     cup water
3       teaspoons sugar
1/4     teaspoon pepper

*Cook bacon until crisp. Drain off as much grease as you can. Add onion and cook 2 minutes. Add all other ingredients except potatoes and cook until just slightly thick. Add sliced potatoes and blend well. Remove from heat and serve warm. Serves 6.*

## Classic Waldorf Salad

2       cups  diced apple
1       cup chopped celery
1/2     cup broken walnuts
1/4     cup mayonnaise
1       tablespoon sugar
1/2     teaspoon lemon juice
        Dash of salt
1/2     cup whipping cream, whipped

*Combine apple, celery, and nuts. Blend mayonnaise, sugar lemon juice, and salt. Fold in whipped cream; fold into apple mixture; chill. Serves 4-6*

# A Taste of
# MAINE
# VEGETABLES

BAR HARBOR SUNSET

## Maine Maple Beans

| | |
|---|---|
| 2 | pounds dry beans |
| 1 | medium onion |
| 1/2 | cup packed brown sugar |
| 1/2 | pound of salt pork |
| 1/2 | teaspoon dry mustard |
| 1/2 | teaspoon ginger |
| 2 | cups dark maple syrup |
| | Salt and pepper to taste |

*Wash the dry beans, place them in a pot, and cover them with water. Let them soak overnight. Drain (reserving liquid) and cover with fresh water. Bring to a boil, and then lower the heat to simmer. Cook until the skins slough off the beans, (approximately one hour). Drain the water off and put it aside. Place the onion in the bottom of a bean pot and pour the beans into the pot. Slice the salt pork almost to the rind in one-half-inch intervals and place it rind side up on top of the beans. In a bowl, mix the maple syrup, dry mustard, ginger, salt, and pepper. Add one cup of the water the beans were cooked in, stir together and pour the mixture over the beans. Add more of the bean water to the pot until it reaches one inch above the beans. Bake in the oven for six to eight hours at 250°. Serves 8-10.*

## Italian Potatoes

| | |
|---|---|
| 2 | cups 1" cubed unpeeled Maine baking potatoes (approx. 3 med.) |
| 3/4 | cup finely chopped onion (1 1/2 med.) |
| 1/2 | cup finely chopped carrot (1 med.) |
| 1/2 | cup low sodium chicken broth |
| 2 | tablespoons tomato paste |
| 1/4 | teaspoon pepper |
| 1/4 | teaspoon salt |
| 2 | cloves garlic, finely chopped |
| 2 | tablespoons chopped parsley |

*Cook all ingredients except parsley in 2 quart saucepan over medium low heat 25-30 minutes. Stirring occasionally, until potatoes are tender. Stir in parsley. Makes 6 servings.*

## Summer Squash Casserole

| | |
|---|---|
| 1 | pound small summer squash |
| 1 | small onion, chopped |
| 3 | tablespoons butter |
| 1 | teaspoon chicken bouillon |
| | Salt and pepper to taste |
| 2 | eggs |
| 2/3 | cup light cream |
| 2/3 | cup grated Gruyere cheese |
| 1 | tablespoon grated Parmesan cheese |

*Preheat oven to 350°. Slice squash and sauté the squash and onion in the butter. Stir in the bouillon. Add salt and pepper to taste. Transfer mixture to a 13"x9" baking pan that has been well greased. Beat eggs, add cream and pour this mixture over the squash. Sprinkle with the cheeses. Bake until lightly browned and set, about 30 minutes. Serves 4.*

## Stuffed Acorn Squash

| | |
|---|---|
| 2 | acorn squash |
| 1/2 | pound bulk sausage |
| 1/2 | cup condensed cream of mushroom soup |
| 3/4 | cup hot water |
| 3 | cups herb stuffing mix |

*Place cleaned squash, cut side face down on cookie sheet. Bake at 350 degrees for 30 minutes. Meanwhile, cook sausage and drain. Mix soup and water. Stir in sausage. Add stuffing mix. Fill squash. Bake at 350 degrees for 30 minutes more or until squash is tender. Serves 4.*

BASS HARBOR LIGHT
Photo: ©William Hammond

# Broccoli Casserole

| | |
|---|---|
| 2 | 10-ounce packages frozen broccoli, cooked and drained |
| 2 | hard-boiled eggs, sliced |
| 2 | cups French-fried onion rings (canned) |
| 2/3 | cup shredded Swiss cheese |
| 2/3 | cup milk |
| 1 | 10.5-ounce can of cream of celery soup |

*Preheat oven to 350°. Arrange the broccoli in a baking pan. Top with the sliced eggs. 1 cup of the onion rings and then the cheese. In a small bowl, mix together the soup and milk. Pour this over the broccoli and bake for 30 minutes. Top with the remaining onion rings and bake for an additional 5-10 minutes.*
*Serves 6.*

## Creamed Spinach with Parmesan Cheese

| | |
|---|---|
| 1/2 | teaspoon butter |
| 2 | packages (10 ounces each) frozen chopped spinach, drained |
| 1 | cup heavy whipping cream |
| 1/2 | cup grated Parmesan cheese |
| 1/2 | teaspoon salt |
| 1/4 | teaspoon freshly ground pepper |
| 1/4 | teaspoon freshly grated nutmeg |
| 1/2 | cup fresh bread crumbs |

*Butter a shallow baking dish. Squeeze as much water as possible from the spinach. Place spinach and cream in a large saucepan and heat over medium high, stirring constantly. Reduce heat and stir in cheese to melt. Add salt, pepper and nutmeg. Adjust seasonings to taste. Transfer spinach mixture to baking dish and sprinkle with breadcrumbs. When ready to serve, place dish in the oven a few inches below the broiler and broil until top is golden and crunchy, about 3 minutes. Makes 6 servings.*

## Hash Brown Potato Casserole

| | |
|---|---|
| 2 | pounds frozen hash brown potatoes |
| 4 | cups grated Cheddar cheese |
| 1 | 10.5-ounce can cream of chicken soup(you can substitute cream of mushroom soup as well) |
| 2 | cups sour cream |
| 1/2 | cup melted butter |
| 1 | medium onion, chopped |
| 1 | teaspoon seasoning salt |

*Preheat oven to 350°. In a large mixing bowl, combine the potatoes, 2 cups of cheese, the soup, sour cream, butter, onion and seasoning. Place into a buttered 13" x 9" x 2" baking pan and bake for 35 minutes. Top with remaining cheese and bake an additional 10-15 minutes. Serves 10.*

## Succotash

| | |
|---|---|
| 1/2 | cup water |
| 2 | tablespoons butter |
| 2 | cups baby lima beans |
| 1 | teaspoon salt |
| | Fresh ground black pepper to taste |
| 1/2 | teaspoon sugar |
| 2 | cups fresh corn, cut off cob |
| 1/3 | cup light cream |

*Bring water and butter to a boil. Add the beans salt, pepper and sugar. Simmer about 12 minutes or until beans are tender. Add the corn and simmer another 4-5 minutes. Stir in the cream. Heat but do not boil. Reseason if needed. Serves 4-6.*

## Lima Beans with Sour Cream

| | |
|---|---|
| 1 | pound large dry lima beans |
| 2 | teaspoons salt |
| 1/3 | cup butter |
| 1 | cup dark corn syrup |
| 1 | teaspoon salt |
| 1 | medium onion, chopped |
| 1 | teaspoon dry mustard |
| 1 | cup sour cream |

*Soak beans and 1 teaspoon salt in 2 1/2 quarts water overnight. Drain and rinse and drain again. Melt butter in a large saucepan. Stir in the syrup and remaining salt. Add beans. Cover and cook over low heat for 50 minutes or until beans are tender. Stir in onion, mustard and sour cream. Turn into a baking pan. Cover and bake in a 350° oven for 1 hour. Serves 6.*

# A Taste of MAINE

# MAIN COURSE
## MEAT & SEAFOOD

WEST QUODDY HEAD LIGHT
*Photo: ©Kevin Shields*

## Boiled Lobster

1    1-2 pound lobster per person
(claws pegged)

*Fill a large kettle half full of water (about 2-3
gallons). Add 1/4 cup salt. Cover and bring to a
full boil. Grasp the lobsters firmly by the middle
of the back with the claws held away. Plunge them
headfirst into boiling water. Cover. Begin counting
cooking time when water again comes to a boil. Cook
15-20 minutes for 1 1/2 – 2 lb. lobsters. Overcook-
ing toughens meat. Plunge cooked lobsters into cold
water for 1 minute to stop cooking process. Twist off
large claws. Make a slit down underside of tail. Serve
with lots of melted butter and lemon.*

## Bouillabaisse

| | |
|---|---|
| 2 | large onions, diced onion |
| 2 | teaspoons minced garlic |
| 1/4 | pound butter |
| 2 | cans clams |
| 1 | bottle clam juice |
| 2 | cups white wine |
| 1 | large can whole plum tomatoes in basil sauce (hand crushed) |
| 2 | tablespoons fennel seed |
| 2 | tablespoons fresh thyme leaves |
| 1 | tablespoon saffron |
| 1 | teaspoon black pepper |
| 1 | teaspoon hot pepper sauce |
| 3 | tablespoons concentrated fish base |
| 2 | pounds assorted fresh fish such as swordfish, shrimp, scallops |
| 8 | each clams and mussels in their shells and |
| 1 | lobster tail |
| | Salt to taste |

*Stock: Sauté onion and garlic in butter until soft-
ened. Add remaining ingredients, except seafood,
and simmer 20 minutes. Quickly sear your assorted
fresh fish in a high heat sauté pan with 1 tablespoon
oil. Add to stock and bring to a simmer. Add 6 to 8
steamed mussels and clams and either half or whole
lobster tail. Allow to simmer for 5 to 10 minutes,
Serve with garlic bread. Serves 6*

## Maine Mussels Steamed in Wine

| | |
|---|---|
| 2 | tablespoons butter |
| 1/4 | cup onion, chopped |
| 2 | cloves garlic, minced |
| 2 | pounds mussels |
| 1/4 | cup white wine |

*In a large saucepan, sauté the onion and garlic in
butter over medium heat for 30 seconds. Add mussels
and wine. Cook approximately 4 minutes, or until
the mussels open. Serve the mussels in bowls with
broth and garnish with a lemon wedge and chopped
parsley. Serve crusty bread for dipping in the broth.
Serves 4.*

## Traditional Finnan Haddie

| | |
|---|---|
| 1 | shallot, chopped |
| 1/4 | cup butter |
| 3 | tablespoons flour |
| 1 | pound Finnan Haddie fillets |
| 1/2 | cup scotch |
| 1 | cup heavy cream |
| 2 | cups fish stock (fish bouillon) |
| 4 | large potatoes, peeled and boiled |

*Skin and chop the Finnan Haddie fillet. Sauté the
fillet and chopped shallot in the butter until the
onions are transparent. Add flour and cook for two
minutes over medium heat. Add scotch and cook an
additional minute to release alcohol. Add heated
fish stock and whisk until smooth. Bring to a boil
and add heated cream. Bring to a boil, lower heat,
and cook slowly to desired consistency. Serve over
warmed, cooked potatoes. Serves 2.*

# Bar Harbor Clambake

| 4 | (1-1/2 pound) live lobsters |
|---|---|
| 8 | ears of shucked corn and/or 8 small potatoes |
| 4 | pounds steamer clams (be sure to soak to remove sand) |
| 1/2 | pound unsalted butter, melted |
| 2 to 3 | pounds Maine Rockweed (seaweed or fresh spinach) |

*Pour 1" of water into a large (20 quart) pot. Divide the green leafy stuff (Rockweed or spinach) into four equal parts. Place one part in the bottom of the pot and place the live lobsters on top. Then cover the lobsters with another layer of green leaves and put the corncobs and/or potatoes) on it. Put a 3rd layer of greens over the and then place your steamer clams over it. Cover the clams with the last layer of rockweed or spinach. Bring the steamer to a boil over high heat, covered, and steam for 30 to 45 minutes, or until the clam shells are all open wide. Serve it up (not the leafy stuff) on four large plates with plenty of real melted butter.*

## Seafood Scampi

| | |
|---|---|
| 1/2 | pound each lobster meat, shrimp, sea scallops |
| 4 | tablespoons butter |
| 1 | tablespoon minced garlic |
| 1 | tablespoon chopped fresh parsley |
| 2 | teaspoons fresh lemon juice |
| 3 | tablespoons dry white wine |
| 1/2 | cup clam juice |
| 2 | tablespoons flour |
| | Salt and pepper |
| 1/4 | cup light cream |
| 4 | additional tablespoons butter |
| 1 | pound cooked fettuccine or spaghetti |

*Cut lobster in bite size pieces and peel and devein shrimp. In a heavy sauté pan melt 4 tablespoons of butter. When the butter begins to bubble add the garlic and shrimp and sauté for about a minute. Next add the scallops and the lobster meat and sauté until the scallops are white and firm. Sprinkle the flour over the seafood while tossing or stirring. Add the clam juice, white wine, parsley, and lemon juice and simmer for about a minute or until the liquid begins to thicken. Add the light cream and return to a simmer. Adjust seasoning and add the additional butter just before serving. Serve over hot pasta. Serves 4*

## Mustard Glazed Salmon

| | |
|---|---|
| 4 | (6 ounce) center-cut salmon fillets |
| 1/4 | teaspoon salt, or to taste |
| | Freshly ground pepper to taste |
| 1/4 | cup reduced-fat sour cream |
| 2 | tablespoons stone-ground mustard |
| 2 | teaspoons lemon juice |
| | Lemon wedges |

*Preheat broiler. Line a broiler pan or baking sheet with foil, then coat it with cooking spray. Place salmon pieces, skin-side down, on the prepared pan. Season with salt and pepper. Combine sour cream, mustard and lemon juice in a small bowl. Spread evenly over the salmon. Broil the salmon 5 inches from the heat source until it is opaque in the center, 10 to 12 minutes. Serve with lemon wedges. Serves 4.*

## Mussels Provencal

| | |
|---|---|
| 4 | pounds mussels |
| 4 | cups white wine |
| 1/2 | cup chopped onions |
| 1 | tablespoon chopped garlic |
| 1 | tablespoon fresh lemon juice |
| 2 | cups chopped tomatoes |

*Place mussels in large soup pot or stockpot. Add all other ingredients. Cover. Cook on high heat and steam until mussels open. Strain mussels into large salad bowl. Reserve liquid. To eat dip mussel meat in reserved cooking liquid. Serves 4-6.*

## Stuffed Maine Lobster

| | |
|---|---|
| 4 | fresh Maine lobsters |
| 1/4 | cup melted butter |
| 2 | tablespoons Worcestershire sauce |
| 1/2 | teaspoon celery salt |
| 2 | tablespoons horseradish |
| 3 | cups crushed crackers or bread crumbs |
| 1 | can minced clams and liquid |
| 1 | jar clam juice |
| 1/4 | teaspoon pepper |
| | Grated cheese (optional) |

*Combine crackers, clams and liquid. Worcestershire sauce, celery salt, pepper, 1/4 cup butter and clam juice. Hold the live lobster firmly and with a large knife cut an opening in the stomach head to tail. Split open. Remove stomach and intestinal vein: discard. Remove greenish tomalley and coral roe (if any) and add to stuffing mixture. Fill each lobster's body cavity with stuffing mixture; place shell side down on broiler pan. Brush with butter. Place in oven on top rack. Bake at 425° for 20 minutes. About five minutes before the lobster is done, you may sprinkle cheese over the stuffing to melt. Lobsters can be prepared ahead of time and cooked when ready.*

# Crab Cakes

1   pound lump crab meat
1   egg, beaten
1/2   cup crushed saltine crackers
1/3   cup minced fresh parsley
2   tablespoons mayonnaise
1/2   teaspoon paprika
Dash of hot sauce
Salt and pepper to taste

*In a medium bowl, toss together lightly the crumbs, egg, parsley and mayonnaise until moistened. Add the crab and seasonings. Mix gently. Form into 6 cakes, 3/4 inch thick. Refrigerate for at least 1 hour to set up. Fry crab cakes in butter in a heavy skillet until both sides and nicely browned, about 10 minutes. Serve immediately.*

## Lobster Cakes

| 6 | slices white bread |
| 3/4 | cup butter, melted |
| 3 | eggs, separated |
| 3 | cups cooked lobster, cut into small chunks |
| 1 | tablespoon finely grated onion, pulp and juice |
| 1 | teaspoon Worcestershire sauce |
| 1/4 | teaspoon dry mustard |
| | Lemon wedges |

Tear bread into small pieces, pour 1/2 cup of the butter over the bread, toss to coat bread. Let stand about 20 minutes or until butter is absorbed. Add egg yolks, lobster, onion, Worcestershire sauce and mustard; mix well. Beat egg whites until stiff; fold into lobster mixture. Shape into 10 patties. In a large skillet, melt remaining 1/4 cup butter. Add patties and cook gently until golden brown on both sides. Serve with lemon wedges. Makes 10 patties.

## Beer-battered Shrimp

| 1/3 | cup all-purpose flour |
| 1/4 | cup beer |
| 1 | large egg white |
| 1/4 | teaspoon salt |
| 3/4 | cup dry bread crumbs |
| 1/4 | cup chopped pecans |
| 1/4 | teaspoon pepper |
| 1/4 | teaspoon salt |
| 1 | pound large shrimp, cleaned peeled and devined |

Preheat oven to 425°. Spray a wire rack with vegetable cooking spray and place on a baking sheet. In a medium bowl, combine flour, beer, egg white and salt; beat until smooth. In another bowl, stir together dry bread crumbs, pecans, pepper, and salt. Dip shrimp in bread crumb mixture, then into the beer batter; dredge a second time in bread crumbs. Set on prepared rack and bake for 12 minutes, or until shrimp have turned pink and coating is golden. Makes 4 servings.

## Portland Baked Scallops

| 12 | jumbo sea scallops |
| 1/2 | cup butter |
| 1 1/2 | cups Italian seasoned bread crumbs |
| 1 | teaspoon lemon juice |
| 1/4 | teaspoon black pepper |
| 1/8 | teaspoon paprika |

Preheat oven to 350°. In small saucepan combine butter, pepper, and lemon. Melt on low heat. Place scallops in medium baking dish. Pour butter mixture over the scallops. Sprinkle breadcrumbs over the top. Sprinkle with small amount of paprika. Bake at 350° for 20 - 30 minutes or until golden brown on top. Serves 3-4.

## Fish & Chips

| 1/2 | cup cornmeal |
| 1/2 | cup flour |
| 4-6 | ounces beer |
| 1/4 | teaspoon salt |
| | Vegetable oil for frying |
| 3 | large russet potatoes, cut into 1/2 in. x 1/2 in. strips |
| 2 | pounds fish fillets, (Cod works well) |
| | Malt vinegar |

Preheat oven to 275°. In a medium bowl, mix the flour, cornmeal and salt together. Add the beer and mix well. The batter should be quite thin. In a deep fryer, fill with oil 1/2 to 2/3 full and heat to 360°. Cook potatoes in 3 batches until golden brown. Drain on paper towels and keep warm in oven while cooking remaining potatoes and fish. Dip fish in batter. Fry in batches until fillets are browned and cooked through, about 5-7 minutes. Drain on paper towels and keep warm in oven until all are cooked. Serve with a sprinkling of malt vinegar. Serves 4

# Swordfish Kabobs

| | | | |
|---|---|---|---|
| 4 | large bamboo skewers | Marinade: | |
| 1 | pound Swordfish steak, cut into 1 to 1 1/2-inch pieces | 1/2 | cup olive oil |
| | | 1 | tablespoon balsamic vinegar |
| 1 | each yellow, green and red pepper, cut into 1-inch pieces | 1 | onion, diced |
| | | 1/2 | teaspoon minced fresh rosemary |
| 4 | large mushrooms, cut into fourths | 1 | small clove garlic, minced |
| | | 1/4 | teaspoon each salt and pepper |
| 1 | red onion, cut into 1-inch pieces | | |
| 1 | zucchini, cut into 1-inch pieces | | |

*Combine all ingredients for marinade in a bowl. Mix well. Set aside. Put all ingredients in the marinade and toss to coat. Let marinate overnight. Put the ingredients on bamboo skewers. (Soak the skewers in water for 20 minutes.) Alternate colors to get best effect. Put the mushrooms on both ends. Grill for 5 minutes on each side or until the swordfish is firm. Serves 4.*

## Seafood Casserole

| | |
|---|---|
| 1 | cup cooked shrimp |
| 1 | cup cooked crab |
| 1 | cup chopped cooked cod |
| 2 | cups soft bread crumbs |
| 2 | cups shredded Cheddar cheese |
| 3 | large eggs |
| 1 1/2 | cups milk |
| 1 | (10.75-ounce) can condensed cream of celery soup |
| 1 | tablespoon Italian seasoning |
| 1/2 | teaspoon salt |
| 1/4 | teaspoon pepper |

*In a medium bowl mix together peeled, cooked shrimp, cooked crab, and cooked, chopped cod. Layer 1 cup soft bread crumbs, grated cheddar cheese, and the seafood mixture in a buttered baking dish. In a small bowl beat eggs and add milk, cream of celery soup, Italian seasoning, salt, and pepper; mix well. Pour over the seafood mixture. Top with remaining soft bread crumbs and the cheddar cheese. Bake in a 325° oven for one hour, or until lightly browned. Makes 4 servings.*

## Clam Fritters

| | |
|---|---|
| 2 | cups steamer clams |
| 2 | cups sifted flour |
| 2 | teaspoons baking powder |
| 1/2 | teaspoon salt |
| 1/4 | teaspoon freshly ground black pepper |
| 1/2 | cup milk, approximately |
| 2 | eggs, separated |
| | Vegetable oil for deep-fat frying |
| | Lemon wedges and parsley for garnish |

*Strain the clams and reserve the liquor. Chop the clams. Prepare the batter by mixing the dry ingredients. Add enough milk to reserved clam liquor to make 1 cup. Stir into dry ingredients. Beat the egg yolks and add to batter. Add the chopped clams. Beat the egg whites until stiff. Fold into clam batter. In a large skillet heat 3 inches of oil to 360°. Drop by tablespoonfuls of batter to hot oil. Do not crowd the pan. Fry until golden and puffed. Turn once. Drain fritters on paper towels and keep warm in a 200° oven until all are cooked. Serves 4.*

## Grilled Citrus Salmon Fillets

| | |
|---|---|
| 1/3 | cup fresh orange juice |
| 1/3 | cup fresh lemon juice |
| 1/3 | cup fresh lime juice |
| 2 | tablespoon brown sugar, packed |
| 1/2 | cup finely chopped onion |
| 2 | tablespoons peeled, finely minced fresh ginger |
| 1/2 | cup fresh cilantro leaves, chopped |
| 6 | (6-ounce center-cut) pieces salmon fillets with skin |
| | Salt and freshly ground black pepper to taste |

*In a blender purée citrus juices, brown sugar, onion and ginger until smooth. Reserve 1/2 cup marinade. Transfer remaining marinade to a large zip-lock style plastic bag and add the cilantro and salmon fillets, seal bag, removing as much air as possible. Marinate salmon in refrigerator for 1 to 2 hours. Prepare grill. Remove salmon from marinade and discard marinade. Pat salmon dry. Season salmon with salt and pepper. Grill, skin side down, on an oiled rack set 5 to 6 inches over glowing coals 4 minutes. Put lid on grill and grill salmon until just cooked through, 3 to 4 minutes more. Carefully transfer salmon with a metal spatula to a platter and remove skin. Pour reserved juice mixture over salmon. Serves 6.*

## Kittery Point Scallops

| | |
|---|---|
| 12 | large scallops cut in fourths |
| 2 | strips bacon |
| 1 | small onion, diced |
| 2 | whole large potatoes, cut into 1-inch cubes |
| 1 | teaspoon flour |
| 1/2 | teaspoon salt |
| 3 | cups heavy cream |
| 1 | tablespoon finely diced red bell pepper |

*Dice bacon. In medium saucepan cook bacon on low heat until bacon is crisp. Add onion. Cook for 2 minutes. Add potatoes and flour and cook for 2 more minutes. Slowly add heavy cream and simmer for 20 minutes. Add scallops and red pepper. Simmer 5 - 8 minutes or until scallops are firm. Serves 6.*

# Duck l'Orange

| | |
|---|---|
| 2 | whole dressed ducks |
| 1 | tablespoons chili powder |
| 1 | tablespoons garlic salt |
| 1 | large Granny Smith apple |
| 2 | garlic cloves |
| 2 | sage leaves |
| 1 | teaspoon light olive oil |
| | L'Orange Sauce (recipe follows) |

*Sprinkle chili powder and garlic salt all over ducks. Cut 1-inch slice in skin of ducks on both sides of breasts. Puree garlic, sage and olive oil and fill in slices in skin with mixture. Chop apple into 1-inch pieces and stuff inside ducks. Bake at 350° for 1 hour and 10 minutes for slightly rare duck meat. Makes 4 servings.*

L'Orange Sauce:

| | |
|---|---|
| 4 | tablespoons mango chutney (Major Greys bottled) |
| 2 | tablespoons peach preserves (low sugar) |
| | Juice of one whole orange |
| 3 | tablespoons of duck drippings from pan |
| 1/4 | cup of dry red wine |

*Put ingredients in saucepan and heat until alcohol simmers off, about 6 minutes. Serve L'Orange sauce over sliced duck. Makes about 1 cup.*

## Apple Chutney Glazed Game Hens

| | |
|---|---|
| 1 | (6-ounce) package long-grain white and wild rice, prepared according to package directions |
| 1 | (8.5-ounce) jar Apple Curry Chutney, divided |
| 1/2 | cup chopped tart green apples |
| 1/4 | cup coarsely chopped almonds |
| 1/4 | cup currants or raisins |
| 1/4 | teaspoon poultry seasoning |
| 1/4 | teaspoon ground ginger |
| 4 | game hens (about 1 1/4 pound each) |
| 1/4 | cup orange juice |
| 3 | tablespoons butter or margarine, melted |

*Preheat oven to 375º F. Combine rice, 1/2 cup chutney, apple, nuts, currants, ginger and poultry seasoning in medium bowl. Spoon about 1 cup stuffing into cavity of each hen. Tie legs together with string; place in 13 x 9-inch baking pan. Bake for 30 minutes. Combine remaining chutney, orange juice and butter in small bowl; brush over hens. Bake, brushing with glaze every 10 minutes, for 40 to 50 minutes or until hens are very well browned and no longer pink near breastbone. Makes 4 servings.*

## Lamb Chops with Fresh Herbs

| | |
|---|---|
| 1/3 | cup vegetable oil |
| 1/3 | cup red wine vinegar |
| 2 | tablespoons soy sauce |
| 1 | tablespoon lemon juice |
| 1 | tablespoon seasoned salt |
| 1/2 | teaspoon each: garlic powder, oregano, rosemary, thyme, marjoram, and dry mustard and white pepper |
| 8 | lamb loin chops (about 2-1/2 pounds) cut 1-inch thick |

*Combine all ingredients, except lamb; mix well. Remove 1/2 of marinade for basting. Place chops in a resealable plastic bag and pour remaining marinade over them. Seal bag and refrigerate for at least 1 hour, turning occasionally. Remove chops from marinade. Discard used marinade. Grill or broil chops until desired doneness, about 8 minutes, turning once and basting often with remaining 1/2 marinade. Discard any remaining marinade. Makes 4 to 6 servings.*

## Venison Pot Roast

| | |
|---|---|
| 1 | large shoulder or rump roast (4-5 lbs) |
| 1 | large onion, chopped |
| 1/4 | cup olive oil |
| 5 | celery stalks, sliced |
| 4 | carrots, sliced |
| 8 - 10 | baby red potatoes |
| 4 | cups beef broth |
| 1 | teaspoon pepper |
| | Salt to taste |
| | Flour enough to thicken broth for a hearty gravy |

*In a large Dutch oven, heat the olive oil and add the chopped onions. Sauté for about 5 minutes and add the roast and braise in the onion and olive oil mixture until browned. If you need to, you can cut the roast into three or four pieces. This makes it easier to turn and brown all sides. When browned, add two cups broth and the rest of the ingredients except for the red potatoes. Now bring to a boil, lower heat, cover and let simmer for about four to five hours. Check every now and then to be sure there is enough liquid and the roast is simmering very slowly, just barely bubbling. Check after the first two hours for tenderness and every hour afterward. When you think the roast is tender enough, add the potatoes and cook until they are done, about 30 minutes. When done, remove the roast and all vegetables and potatoes -- just leaving the juices in the pot. Now take the last two cups of the cold broth and mix well with the flour, about 1/2 cup, adding the flour slowly. Add this to the juices in the pot and keep stirring until a thick, rich gravy is made. Put the cooked roast with the potatoes and vegetables on a large serving plate and the gravy in a separate bowl and serve.*

BULL MOOSE
*Photo: ©Robert Villani*

# A Taste of
# MAINE
# BREADS &
# DESSERTS

BLUEBERRY FIELD
Photo: ©Gary Stanley

## Apple Brown Betty

| | |
|---|---|
| 1/2 | cup butter, softened |
| 1/2 | cup rolled oats |
| 1/2 | cup flour |
| 3/4 | cup brown sugar (packed) |
| 1/2 | teaspoon nutmeg |
| 1 | teaspoon cinnamon |
| 1/4 | cup water |
| 4 | cups of apples, peeled and sliced (I recommend using Courtland or similar apples) |

Combine the brown sugar, oats, cinnamon, nutmeg, flour, and butter and stir with a fork until well mixed and crumbly. Add one third of the apples, then one third of the crumb mixture to a greased, 1 1/2-quart baking dish. Repeat until all apples and crumb mixture are added. Pour the 1/4 cup of water over the mixture. Bake for 30 minutes in a preheated 375° oven. Serve warm with vanilla ice cream. Serves 6

## Maine Apple Cake

*Any type of apple can be used in this recipe, but it's great with fresh McIntosh apples!*

| | |
|---|---|
| 3 1/2 | cups milk |
| 4 1/2 | cups finely diced apples |
| 1/2 | cup vegetable oil |
| 2 | cups flour |
| 2 | cups sugar |
| 3/4 | cup chopped walnuts |
| 2 | eggs, beaten |
| 2 | teaspoons vanilla |
| 2 | teaspoons baking soda |
| 2 | teaspoons cinnamon |
| 1/2 | teaspoon salt |

Mix apples and sugar together. Add beaten eggs, oil, nuts, and vanilla. In separate bowl, mix remaining dry ingredients together and add to apple mixture. Bake in a greased 13x9" inch pan for 60 minutes at 350 degrees.

## Chocolate Mayonnaise Cake

| | |
|---|---|
| 1 1/2 | cups sugar |
| 1 1/2 | cups mayonnaise (Miracle Whip works too) |
| 1 1/2 | cups water |
| 1 1/2 | teaspoons vanilla |
| 3 | cups flour |
| 2/3 | cups cocoa |
| 2 1/4 | teaspoons baking powder |
| 1 1/2 | teaspoons baking soda |

Preheat oven to 350° F. Cream together first four ingredients. Add remaining ingredients and stir until well mixed. Pour into greased 9 x 13" pan. Bake in preheated oven for 35-40 minutes or until a toothpick inserted in center of cake comes out clean.

## Pumpkin Pie

| | |
|---|---|
| 1 1/4 | cups pumpkin puree |
| 3/4 | cup sugar |
| 1/2 | teaspoon salt |
| 1/4 | teaspoon ground ginger |
| 1 | teaspoon ground cinnamon |
| 1 | teaspoon flour |
| 2 | eggs, lightly beaten |
| 1 | cup evaporated milk |
| 2 | tablespoons water |
| 1/2 | teaspoon vanilla extract |
| 1 | unbaked 9-inch pastry shell |

Preheat oven to 400°. Combine pumpkin, sugar, salt, spices and flour in a medium-sized mixing bowl. Add eggs and mix well. Add evaporated milk, water and vanilla. Mix well. Pour into pastry-lined pie pan. Bake at 400° for 15 minutes, reduce heat to 350° and bake 35 minutes longer or until center is set. Serves 6

# Blueberry Streusel Muffins

| | |
|---|---|
| 1 | cup milk |
| 1/4 | cup vegetable oil |
| 1/2 | teaspoon vanilla |
| 1 | large egg |
| 2 | cups all-purpose flour |
| 1/3 | cup sugar |
| 3 | teaspoons baking powder |
| 1/2 | teaspoon salt |
| 1 | cup fresh or canned (drained) blueberries |

Topping:

| | |
|---|---|
| 2 | tablespoons butter |
| 1/4 | cup all-purpose flour |
| 2 | tablespoons packed brown sugar |
| 1/4 | teaspoon ground cinnamon |

*Preheat oven to 400°. Grease bottoms of 12 muffin cups or use paper cup liners. Prepare the topping by thoroughly blending the 4 ingredients in a small bowl. Set aside. Beat the milk, oil, vanilla and egg in a bowl. Add the dry ingredients until flour is just moistened. Fold in the blueberries. Divide the batter among the 12 muffin cups. Sprinkle each with about 2 teaspoons topping. Bake for 20-25 minutes in preheated oven. Immediately remove from muffin tins and cool on a rack. Serve warm.*

# Fried Dough

| | |
|---|---|
| 1/2 | cup milk |
| 3/4 | cup water |
| 1 | tablespoon vegetable oil |
| 1 | teaspoon salt |
| 1/4 | cup sugar |
| 3 | cups flour |
| 2 | teaspoons yeast |
| | Oil for frying |

*Mix vigorously in a large mixing bowl and let rise until double in bulk. Turn the dough out onto a floured surface. Punch down and knead. Roll out to about 1/8 inch thick. Cut into strips 2-inches wide and cut the strips into squares. Cover and let rest for about 10 minutes. Using a large fry pan, fill with about three inches of cooking oil. Heat until the temperature of the oil is 360 degrees. If the fat is too cool, the dough will absorb the oil and if the fat is too hot, the dough will brown before it is cooked in the middle. Lower the dough gently into the cooking oil, two or three pieces at a time. When brown on one side, turn and brown on the other side. Lift from the cooking oil with a fork or tongs and drain on paper towels. Brush the fried dough with melted butter and sprinkle with powdered or cinnamon sugar.*

# Dinner Rolls

| | |
|---|---|
| 4 | cups flour |
| 1 | package rapid-rise yeast |
| 1/3 | cup sugar |
| 1 | teaspoon salt |
| 1 | cup milk |
| 1/2 | cup butter |
| 3 | large egg yolks |

*Using an electric mixer, whisk together in the bowl the flour, yeast, sugar and salt. In a small saucepan, heat the milk and butter, stirring until the butter melts and the liquid is very warm (about 120°). Pour the warm milk mixture along with the egg yolks into the flour mixture. Using a dough hook, mix until all is well blended. Remove dough from bowl and knead several minutes, adding more flour if dough is still sticky. Lightly grease the sides of a large bowl, place dough in bowl, place in bowl and cover with plastic wrap or towel. Let rise in a warm spot until doubled in size (about 1 hour). Lightly grease a 9" x 13" baking pan. Turn dough out onto a floured work surface. Divide dough into 16 equal pieces. Form into smooth balls and place in pan with any seams on the bottom.*

# Baked Indian Pudding

| | |
|---|---|
| 1 1/2 | quarts milk |
| 1 | cup yellow cornmeal |
| 1/2 | cup dark molasses |
| 1/4 | cup sugar |
| 1/4 | cup butter |
| 1/2 | teaspoon salt |
| 1/4 | teaspoon baking powder |
| 2 | eggs, slightly beaten |
| | Whipped cream or ice cream |

*Preheat oven to 500°. Prepare a 13" x 9" baking pan by greasing it well. Using half the hot milk (3 cups) combine and thoroughly mix all ingredients except the whipped cream or ice cream. Pour into the baking dish. Bake until pudding comes to a boil. Then stir in the remaining milk. Reduce heat to 200° and bake the pudding for 5-6 hours. Serve warm with whipped cream or vanilla ice cream. Serves 10-12*

# Hot Fudge Pudding Cake

| | |
|---|---|
| 1 1/2 | cups flour |
| 1 1/4 | cups sugar |
| 3 | tablespoons cocoa |
| 3 | teaspoons baking powder |
| 1/2 | teaspoon salt |
| 3/4 | cup milk |
| 3 | tablespoons vegetable shortening |

*Mix all the above ingredients together and spread in a greased 9 x 13" pan.*

Mix Together:

| | |
|---|---|
| 1 | cups brown sugar |
| 1/3 | cup cocoa |
| 2 | cups hot water |

*Mix ingredients together. Carefully pour mixture over the batter in the cake pan. Do not stir. Bake at 350 degrees for 1 hour.*

# Lemon Cream Cheese Pound Cake

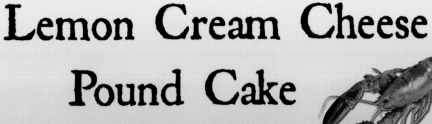

| | |
|---|---|
| 1 1/2 | cups butter |
| 1 | (8 oz.) cream cheese, softened |
| 3 | cups sugar |
| 6 | eggs, at room temperature |
| 2 | teaspoons vanilla |
| 1/2 | teaspoon salt |
| 3 | cups flour |
| 1 | teaspoon baking powder |
| 1 | cup buttermilk |
| 2 | teaspoons lemon zest |

*Preheat oven to 325°. Cream together the first 3 ingredients. Add eggs, one at a time. Beat after each addition. Add vanilla. Blend in flour, salt and baking powder alternating dry ingredients with the buttermilk. Pour into greased and floured tube or bundt pan. Bake at 325 degrees for 1 hour and 15 minutes. Serves 12*

## Maple Raisin Bread

| | |
|---|---|
| 1/2 | cup milk |
| 1/4 | cup butter |
| 1/4 | cup Maine maple syrup |
| 1 | tablespoon dry yeast |
| 2 | eggs |
| 1/4 | cup dry milk powder |
| 1/2 | cup wheat germ |
| 1/2 | cup raisins |
| 3 1/4 | cups all purpose flour |
| | Cinnamon and maple sugar for topping |

*For the filling: In a large bowl, mix together the maple sugar mixed with one teaspoon cinnamon. Add the butter. Scald the milk in a cup in the microwave or in a saucepan on top of the stove and pour over the butter mixture. Add the raisins and wheat germ. Stir until butter is melted and the temperature of the mixture is less than 110 degrees. (A temperature higher than this will kill the yeast). Add the eggs, yeast, milk powder and flour. Mix with a dough hook until dough forms a ball. Remove the dough from the bowl and knead well. On a well-floured surface, roll the dough into a 16-inch by 10-inch rectangle. Sprinkle the dough generously with a mixture of cinnamon and maple sugar. Roll the dough into a loaf, and place in a well-greased 5 x 9" loaf pan. Let the bread rise until double in bulk, about 90 minutes.*

*Preheat the oven to 350 degrees. Bake the bread until nicely brown and the loaf has a hollow sound when tapped, about 35 minutes. Remove from pan and let cool on a rack before slicing.*

## Easy Maple Nut Fudge

| | |
|---|---|
| 3 | cups pure maple syrup |
| 1 | cup milk |
| 1/2 | cup chopped nuts |

*Butter an 8-inch square baking dish; set aside. Combine maple syrup and milk in a heavy saucepan. Boil mixture, stirring occasionally, to the softball stage, or 238°F (115°C) on the candy thermometer. Remove from heat and cool to lukewarm without stirring. With a heavy wooden spoon, beat until mixture starts to become thickened and creamy. Stir in nuts. Pour mixture into prepared baking pan, spreading mixture out evenly. Score with knife. Let cool until firm and cut into pieces. Store in airtight container in a cool place. Makes about 1 1/4 pounds.*

## Blueberry Frozen Yogurt

| | |
|---|---|
| 2 | cups lemon-lime flavored soda, chilled |
| 2 | cups blueberries |
| 1/2 | cup sugar |
| 2 | teaspoons lemon juice |
| 16 | ounces nonfat vanilla yogurt |

*Place soda, blueberries, sugar, lemon juice in a blender; process until smooth. Combine blueberry mixture and yogurt. Pour into a baking dish and then in the freezer. When frozen, serve in individual dessert dishes. Serves 4-6.*

## Cranberry Bread

| | |
|---|---|
| | Juice and grated peel of 1 orange |
| | Boiling water |
| 2 | tablespoons butter |
| 1 | cup sugar |
| 1 | egg |
| 1 | cup chopped fresh cranberries |
| 1/2 | cup chopped walnuts |
| 2 | cups flour |
| 1/2 | teaspoon salt |
| 1/2 | teaspoon baking soda |
| 1/2 | teaspoon baking powder |

*Preheat oven to 325°. Put orange juice in a 1 cup measure. Add enough boiling water to make 3/4 cup. Add the grated peel and butter. Stir until butter is melted. Set aside. In a mixing bowl, beat sugar and egg together; add the orange mixture and stir until well blended. Add the cranberries and nuts. Sift together the flour, salt, baking soda, and baking powder. Stir into the egg mixture. Pour into a greased 9"x5"x3" loaf pan. Bake in preheated oven for about 1 hour or until a toothpick inserted in center comes out clean. Cool and store overnight before serving.*

MOUNT KATHADIN
Photo: ©Kevin Shields